T0194812

LIFE *in the* HANDS *of* JESUS

Sharmila Panirselvam

WESTBOW
P R E S S®
A DIVISION OF THOMAS NELSON
& ZONDERVAN

WestBow Press books may be ordered through
booksellers or by contacting:

WestBow Press
A Division of Thomas Nelson & Zondervan
1663 Liberty Drive
Bloomington, IN 47403
www.westbowpress.com
844-714-3454

ISBN: 978-1-6642-5952-2 (sc)
ISBN: 978-1-6642-5951-5 (e)

Library of Congress Control Number: 2022904278

Print information available on the last page.

WestBow Press rev. date: 03/08/2022

CONTENTS

JESUS, I LOVE YOU

I am a living testimony, dear reader, that Jesus is everything in me. Why do I boldly say that? Let me explain. For many years, I have been a single woman, yet now, at the age of forty-seven, I dare to say that the Lord is the lover of my soul. He became my other half, what others may call husband. Does this mean I have no desire to marry? The answer is simple: no! I knew many men when I was younger, but deep inside, I felt something was missing, which made me search for more profound, more meaningful things in life. Life was a mystery because I did not know the purpose of being born into this world. At night in my bed, I asked the question, *Where did all the dead people go?* I had seen many deaths in my early teenage journey. Would my God talk to me? Was God responsible for my life and death? Life was so unfair because my loved ones would die someday. I dearly loved my parents very much.

I saw the sacrifice of my mother waking up early to make breakfast and getting her children ready for school. My dad ensured his kids were safe on the school bus, and he would prepare to go to work after that. Why all this sacrifice of love, when they would die and leave their kids behind? In my teenage years, I was an insecure child. Whenever I went to bed at the time, I felt depressed inside. There were many nights my pillow was wet with tears, as I thought about how unfair life was. Each time I played with my siblings, I realized that one day I would not play with them anymore. It seemed everything was just temporary.

In my early teenage years, I was seriously looking for the meaning of life. I used to see my dad praying every evening. We were Hindu; we had an altar with gods and goddesses that we prayed to. I followed my dad, praying daily, kneeling at the altar, and making a big prayer. I asked God to talk to me and to show me His real face. Our Hindu altar has many goddesses' picture and a few statues. Daily I prayed the same thing. My dad also taught us how to pray, and he taught us about God from the Hindu book called *Mahabharata*. Yet, I felt God did not hear my prayer. He was far away, and I felt all my prayers were in vain.

Around the age of seventeen, I started my journey on finding God, the meaning of life, and answers to the questions of why humans must go through death, why I had emotions, and why I needed emotions. I felt life would be much better without emotion because I would not be bothered with the feelings of love and hate. Amid that, many life changes took place. I completed high school, went into nursing college at age twenty, and started working at age twenty-three. I knew I should get married at some point in my life, have kids of my own, and grow my own family. Meanwhile, the search for God continued. As a Hindu, every Friday I attended the temple for prayers. I never failed to ask God to talk to me, and this time I requested that He lead me to the right man for my marriage.

It was a long, long journey before I encountered Jesus

and realized that He is the one true living God. One touch of His presence changed everything in my life, and I pursued Him like a lover I had long waited for in this lifetime. Once I came to know the one true God, I was occupied in knowing Him. I remained a single woman because Jesus was everything at that time. Does this mean I am asking you to be single, like me? The answer is no! Each person is created in the image of God (Genesis 1:26–27), and God has a plan for you (Jeremiah 29:11). He puts His spiritual gifts (Ephesians 4:7) in you to accomplish His will on this earth. It is wise to follow God's path for you to have a blessed life on this earth.

I do not see myself as anything less than others, and I do not compare myself to others. When I was younger and searching, I did compare myself many times and nearly lost my self-confidence. I felt less beautiful, less intelligent, and unable to communicate fluently. I compared myself to others in many ways, each of which greatly depressed me. Meanwhile, I was also interested in the more profound things in life, such as why I was born, why some people are born blind and deaf or without arms and legs, why some people live without food and shelter or suffer from sickness and diseases in their bodies, and so many more. When I saw those less fortunate in their physical appearance, I knew I was blessed to be born in a perfect shape, with nothing lacking. At night in my bed, I pondered the existence of God and grieved for the less fortunate people. Long story short: if you have read my testimony from my first book, *In Search of Deeper Things in Life*, you will know how I met the Lord Jesus. I have been in love with the Lord ever since, and the love story continues in this book.

I am fearfully and wonderfully made by my Lord (Psalm 139:14). Even though my parents came together to conceive me in my mother's womb, my Heavenly Father already knew me before He formed me (Jeremiah 1:5). He knew when I would be born, where I would be born, how I would look, what I would do on this earth, and everything about me, because He is omnipotent, omnipresent, and omniscient. Above all, He is the Creator of Heaven and Earth. The deep search I went on to understand life and death when I was a teenager led me to the Lord Jesus. I was thirty-four years old when I came to know the Lord and started my new life as a born-again woman.

MY EARLY LIFE

In my mid- and late twenties, I deeply desired to marry, yet I was in a conflict at the same time. I was unsatisfied with my life and filled with anxiety about death and dying. I craved an answer for human suffering and why we human beings are created unequally—some with defective features, some sick, some starving and without food, some homeless, some orphaned, and some with many more conditions that I mourned in my heart.

Being born and raised a Hindu, I constantly begged God to talk to me and answer all these burning questions. I wanted to know God and to feel His presence here on earth. I sensed God was far away and unable to hear me. I took the initiative to read the Hindu scripture *Mahabharata*, but gained truly little understanding from the book. Eventually, a Chinese friend introduced me to Taoism. I told my Chinese friend I wanted to know God. She was exceedingly kind; she explained that God would manifest Himself in the form of light. She took me to the Taoist temple. I prayed fervently, kneeling at the altar and asking God to talk to me and manifest Himself to me. My friend gave me a book containing stories of people who had seen God and been surrounded by the light. I was fascinated by that, hoping that I would have the same experience if I persisted in my prayer. I became a vegetarian as well because Taoism is against killing animals or any kind of living being. I told my dad about Taoism, shared the book with him, and made him aware that I was a vegetarian. My dad was displeased by that. He said I was living under his roof and that I should obey my parents' religion and eat everything my mom cooked. I listened to my dad and let go of Taoism.

Yet my heart was still in a searching mode, and I did not give up. I was seventeen then. Since I was surrounded by a Muslim population of more than 50 percent living in Malaysia, I thought Islam must be the one true religion that would ensure my soul was safe and that I would be with God when I died. Despite living under my parents' roof, I secretly listened to my Muslim friends at school about their belief system. I stayed in the classroom while Islam was being taught. Non-Muslim students were given a choice: they could either go to the library during that lesson or remain in the classroom; those who stayed in the classroom worked on the other homework. Most of the time, I stayed in the classroom. The secondary school I went to consisted of 90 percent Muslim students. The teacher who taught Islam would touch on all the other faiths globally and conclude that Islam was the one true religion and Allah was the one and only God that existed in this universe. I saw them praying five times per day and fasting for thirty days (about four and a half weeks) during the Ramadhan month. I was convinced that Allah was the true God that one should serve. I kept it to myself. I did not tell my dad this because I was still living under his roof. If I told my dad, he would not be pleased, and that would cause him heartache and altogether destroy my pursuit of Allah. I said to myself, *I will convert to Islam when I am not under my parent's watch—that is when I am old, and before I die—I will be with God after my death.*

Somehow though, it was strange that I lost interest in knowing more about Islam and Allah, even though I had many Muslim friends. I was not eager to ask them much about Allah anymore. Life went on in my deeper search for inner satisfaction. Malaysia has about 9 percent of the global Christian population. I had heard about Jesus and had seen people going from house to house, giving away a booklet called *Jesus Is Lord*. I never paid attention to it; it seemed like Jesus was a commercialized God. People needed to advertise Him to get the attention and to influence others to follow Him. I wasn't a bit interested in that.

I went through my early life like most adults. I completed college and became a nurse. I worked as a staff nurse, and I remain a nurse to this day. When I began earning money, I traveled around, barhopped with friends, dined in fancy restaurants, and helped my parents. I loved and adored them, and remembered all the sacrifices they made when I was a child. Now and then, in my early life, I was frightened of my parents passing away and wondered where they would be after leaving this earth. When I lay in bed at night, I asked myself these questions: *Would someone be there for them? What would happen to my parents after they passed on?*

Life continued with unanswered questions, and I went on doing what was required in life. I worked, enjoying the money I earned by sharing activities I liked with my parents and friends. After five years of service in one of the hospitals in Malaysia, my place of birth, I left for Saudi Arabia and worked there for six years as a staff nurse. I made more money and increased my knowledge and skills. While I was in Saudi Arabia, I began reading self-help books like *The Subconscious Mind*, *The Secret*, *Chicken Soup for the Soul*, and many others.

I was feeling dull in my heart; reading these self-help books kept me alive on the inside. Each book helped for a while, yet still I found something missing deep inside me. I yearned to know God and whether He could be reached. I discovered Trinity Broadcasting Channel (TBN) while working in Saudi Arabia. Preachers like Joel Osteen, Joyce Meyer, and Charles Stanley helped me gain a positive mindset; still, I rejected that Jesus was the only way. When Pastor Charles Stanley was about to close his sermon with a prayer, I would shut off the television, doing the same when Pastor Joel Osteen asked the audience to receive Jesus into their hearts. Once again, I told myself, *These people are advertising Jesus, and I don't need Jesus in my life to be successful.* I never bothered to know Jesus at that time. I wanted to know whether God was here on earth, not listen to some men telling me that Jesus is God, that people must listen to that and accept it. I was desperate and hungry for God Himself to tell me face-to-face that He was God, and He would be there when I died.

After six years in Saudi Arabia, I moved to the United States. Despite being busy sorting out a new workplace, unfamiliar environment, and new people, I was ready to start my spiritual journey in California. I searched on Google for a Hinduism class, desiring to find a one-to-one coach who could teach me about God and how I could connect to Him. I was still searching, and still a Hindu at that time. I planned to get private teaching lessons to understand God and the universe's existence.

While doing my search for a class, I made a few new friends at work. In short, I ended up being in church one Sunday evening. I never expected this; my friend and I were supposed to have dinner in a restaurant that Sunday evening. This friend of mine neglected to tell me that she and her husband would drop by their church before dinner. My friend explained that we would be there just for a short time, then proceed to dinner. I was disappointed with my friend and felt humiliated, believing she disrespected me for being a Hindu. In my book *In Search of Deeper Things in Life,* I share more detail on how I fell in love with the Lord Jesus while in the church that night, despite my anger. I received Jesus into my heart right away; my heart was changed instantly. Suddenly, I wanted to know about Jesus and to attend church every Sunday with my friend. I have been converted ever since. That was the greatest miracle that ever happened to me: I had met God, He answered all my provocative questions, and fulfilled my desperation and hunger for Him, a desire I had felt since I was a teenager.

MY LORD JESUS
WORKED ON ME

For everything, there is a time (Ecclesiastes 3:1), and the Lord makes everything beautiful in His own time (Ecclesiastes 3:11). My search for God finally ended at the feet of Jesus. Everything happens in His ordained time. I say that because I had heard about Jesus via television. At the time, I did not believe that He was the one true God, but when I listened to the Gospel preached by a pastor, and had my personal experience in church, it changed everything. It was perfect timing because I had a church to learn about my savior and to grow in faith within its community.

When I found God, I found my lover, and I wanted to know that person more every day. I start reading the Bible; in my journey, I began in the New Testament because that is where Jesus walked on earth with His disciples. Every word that Jesus spoke in the Bible penetrated my heart. It seemed like the Word was alive and was doing something in my heart and mind. In Hebrew 4:12, the scripture says, "For the word of God is living and powerful, and sharper than any two-edged sword, piercing even to the division of soul and spirit, and joint and marrow, and is a discerner of the thoughts and intents of the heart." I started to see things from the perspective of the Lord Jesus. I had a brand-new life, I changed how I thought, and everything I did was to please my lover.

When I received Jesus in my heart, I had no idea that I was born again. Being born again is also known as spiritual rebirth, or a regeneration of a human spirit by the Holy Spirit, in contrast with physical birth. You receive the Holy Spirit when you accept Jesus into your heart for the first time, and the Holy Spirit makes you a born-again person in Christ Jesus. You develop a direct and personal relationship with God, and that relationship is with the Lord Jesus.

The first birth that a human has is a fleshly birth, where a mother gives birth to a child from her physical body. The baby's creation in the mother's womb is from two human beings: the male and the female. To see the spiritual world, one must be born in the Spirit. As Jesus explained clearly in John 3:5–7, "Most assuredly, I say to you unless one is born again, he cannot see the kingdom of God." Later in this passage, the ruler of the Jews, Nicodemus, asked Jesus, "How can a man be born when he is old? Can he enter a second time into his mother's womb and be born?" Jesus answered, "Most assuredly, I say to you, unless one is born of water and the Spirit, he cannot enter the kingdom of God. That which is born of the flesh is flesh, and that which is born of the Spirit is Spirit. Do not marvel that I said to you, 'You must be born again.'"

It was like I returned to being a baby in the hands of Jesus. Daily I read His words. I asked for clarification from my pastor. I prayed for His plans and purpose to be revealed. I worshipped Him and spent time meditating on

His words and His ways. I asked the Holy Spirit to give me an understanding of the Word and the ways of Jesus, because the Holy Spirit is God Himself living inside me, and ultimately, He is the teacher who takes precedent over all the knowledge that I receive from people explaining the scripture to me.

As the days passed, I became more in love with my savior. I could see He was doing magnificent work in me, and the transformation could be seen in the way I lived my life. *Wow, what a savior He is,* I thought. I marveled at how a heart could be changed in His presence. I shared the good news with my parents. I told them that Jesus is the one true living God. There was no resistance or anger or disappointment, but instead my dad was happy for me. He said that I had chosen to follow a godly man in my life. My parents knew Jesus as a good man who followed God and not as God. My dad told me as a Hindu, God was with him, and he would remain a Hindu. Ever since, I have been praying daily for every one of my family members to be touched one day. I wanted them to have eternal life with Jesus. I left that in the hands of God, because there is a perfect time for everything. I do get worried about my parents, but somehow there is peace and confidence after prayer that they will come to Jesus one day. I continued my journey with the Lord.

Even though I was already in my thirties when I was saved, it was not too late, and I decided not to waste another second without Jesus being my lover. My lover was everything in my life. I held Him close to me, though I frequently forgot that He was alive in me. It was fascinating to know that God was living inside me. *Wow,* I thought, *not even a husband would be able to live inside me, but God can.* And that is why I fell intimately in love with Jesus. My Lord transformed my life to shine brighter and created more remarkable changes in me that no human could ever have performed. Wow! What a God He is!

Being with Jesus made me speak differently, treat people with kindness, honor my parents, respect all authorities, exercise honesty, work hard, take responsibility in money matters, continue pursuing higher education, and choose the right food and drink for my health. By doing so, I brought glory to God. In 1 Corinthians 10:31, the scripture says, "Therefore, whether you eat or drink, or whatever you do, do all to the glory of God."

DEEPER WORKS IN ME

As I seek more of the Lord daily, He brings me deeper into understanding Him and His marvelous ways. Jesus is full of compassion. The compassion that He had for people enabled him to heal the sick, open blind eyes and deaf ears, raise the dead, and cast out demons. Besides being a man, Jesus is also 100 percent God, and therefore full of God's power within Him—power that enables Him to raise a dead person. He is full of love and sensitivity toward people's needs. Since He was also a man, He was filled with the Holy Spirit, which allowed Him to do the works of God.

I was amazed at what Jesus did for the people who came to Him with bodily illness and demonic possession. Jesus also said that more significant works than this His disciples would do (John 14:12). I believe those who follow Jesus today are His disciples and will continue doing the mighty works of God through the power of the Holy Spirit. Apostle Paul said in 1 Corinthians 2:4, "And my speech and my preaching were not with persuasive words of human wisdom, but in demonstration of the spirit and of power."

In my early teenage years, I grieved over the less fortunate people I saw around me. I felt hopeless and useless because I

hink, *How*
ture look
to me

...en I saw the blind and deaf. My
without an answer to my questions. I
nat Jesus did for the blind and deaf whom
...cross. In John 9:1–6 the Lord opened a blind
...'s eyes.

Now as Jesus passed by, He saw a man who was blind
from birth. And His disciples asked Him, saying, "Rabbi,
who sinned, this man or his parents, that he was born
blind?" Jesus answered, "Neither this man nor his parents
sinned, but that the works of God should be revealed in
him. I must work the works of Him who sent Me while it is
day; the night is coming when no one can work. As long as
I am in the world, I am the light of the world." When He
had said these things, He spat on the ground and made clay
with the saliva; and He anointed the eyes of the blind man
with the clay. And He said to him, "Go, wash in the pool of
Siloam" (which is translated, Sent). So he went and washed,
and came back seeing.

In Mark 7:32–35, the Lord Jesus opened deaf ears.

Then they brought to
deaf and had an impedim
and they begged Him to
on him. And He took him a
multitude, and put His fingers
and He spat and touched his tong
looking up to heaven, He sighed,
to him, "Ephphatha," that is, "Be op
Immediately his ears were opened, and
impediment of his tongue was loosed, a
he spoke plainly.

As for the widows and orphans, the Lord want
people to care for them. In James 1:27, the scripture s
"Pure and undefiled religion before God and the Father
this: to visit orphans and widows in their trouble, and to
keep oneself unspotted from the world."

I discovered that the heart of the Lord is for the
unfortunate. The Lord Jesus healed many who were sick
and came to him for healing. After Jesus was crucified, the
disciples of Jesus continued to carry out the works of Jesus
by healing many who needed healings in their bodies. In
Matthew 10:7–8 the Lord Jesus gave these instructions to
His disciples: "And as you go, preach, saying, 'The kingdom
of heaven is at hand.' Heal the sick, cleanse the lepers, raise
the dead, cast out demons. Freely you have received, freely
give." From this scripture, I understood that we born-
again Christians should be the hands and feet for Jesus in
spreading the Gospel, praying for the sick, and helping the
poor and the orphans. My agony for the less fortunate slowly
decreased because now I knew I could pray for the healing

for their sick bodies and their broken hearts, and render godly mission services or give financial support whenever possible to reduce their burdens.

I hunger for more of my Lord. I wanted to speak in tongues, as the apostle Paul did in the Bible. I finally received that gift during my twenty-one days of fasting and prayer some years back. I was persistent and pressed into the Lord during those twenty-one days. Since then, I can pray in a known language and in my unknown language, which I call the spirit language. Each time, I feel satisfied and at peace after my prayer. It is like I am sailing higher with Jesus. The scripture in 1 Corinthians 14:2 says, "For he who speaks in a tongue does not speak to men but God, for no one understands him; however, in the spirit, he speaks mysteries." One thing is sure: the more I know the Lord, the hungrier I get and the more I want of Him. It is like an addiction that I ask for, yet more and more is still not enough. What a Lord He is that makes His beloved want more of Him.

I have seen blind eyes open with my own eyes. That was exciting! Jesus is the same yesterday, today, and forever (Hebrews 13:8). I wrote in great length in my first book about this miracle. I have also experienced warmth in church services during worship and in my private prayer meetings with Christian friends. It is always special when the Lord shows up by warming you from the inside out. I also experience tapping on my shoulders and pulsating in my hands and feet during worship. He is a God who is not dormant but alive, and He wants you to know that He is there when everyone in one accord is calling upon Him and worshipping Him. The Lord Jesus said in Matthew 18:20,

"For where two or three are gathered together in My name, I am there in the midst of them."

As I went deeper, I desperately yearned for spiritual gifts in my life. I sought the Lord daily and never neglected to ask for this. Even though I was speaking in tongues, I wanted a spiritual gift I could use, both in the church and out of the church. I started to pray for anyone who needed comfort and healing in their body. I always experienced peace in my heart whenever I prayed for people. They may not have been instantly healed from their sickness, but certainly their hearts were softened, and I trusted they would fall in love with Jesus. Jesus's heart is for the repentance of sin, and He came for the broken-hearted. When I saw a wounded heart begin to cry, and hoped they were being comforted by Jesus through my prayers, it reminded me of the scripture in Isaiah 61:1–2:

> The Spirit of the Lord is upon Me; Because the Lord has anointed Me; To preach good tidings to the poor; He has sent me to heal the brokenhearted; To proclaim liberty to the captives; And the opening of the prison to those who are bound; To proclaim the acceptable year of the Lord, And the day of vengeance of our God; To comfort all who mourn.

The scripture means the spirit of the Lord is upon Jesus, and He is the anointed one who came to heal the broken-hearted, comfort all who mourn, to preach the good news to the poor, to proclaim liberty to the enslaved, and to set us free from our sin.

If comforting others through my prayers was a gift, then I would use it with faith. The gift of exhortation and mercy is mentioned in Romans 12:8. The Lord knows the perfect spiritual gifts for His saints. The gifts of exhortation and mercy fit me well because of my job as a nurse rendering care for my patients. The Lord knows the best spiritual gifts that fit each of us well, and He distributes them according to His choice. There is nothing wrong with asking for more gifts, such as the working of miracles, healing, administration, and many more that can be found in Romans 12:1 Corinthians 12, and Ephesians 4. Let me write down the gifts from each scripture that I mention here, so you will know the different spiritual gifts that God can put in us to fulfill His mission on earth.

> For as we have many members in one body, but all the members do not have the same function, so we, being many, are one body in Christ, and individually members of one another. Having then gifts differing according to the grace that is given to us, let us use them: if prophecy, let us prophesy in proportion to our faith; or ministry, let us use it in our ministering; he who teaches, in teaching; he who exhorts, in exhortation; he who gives, with liberality; he who leads, with diligence; he who shows mercy, with cheerfulness. (Romans 12:4–8)

There are diversities of gifts, but the same Spirit. There are differences of ministries, but the same Lord. And there are diversities of activities, but it is the same God who works all in all. But the manifestation of the Spirit is given to each one for the profit of all: for to one is given the word of wisdom through the Spirit, to another the word of knowledge through the same Spirit, to another faith by the same Spirit, to another gifts of healings by the same Spirit, to another the working of miracles, to another prophecy, to another discerning of spirits, to another different kinds of tongues, to another the interpretation of tongues. But one and the same Spirit works all these things, distributing to each one individually as He wills. (1 Corinthians 12:4–11)

And He Himself gave some to be apostles, some prophets, some evangelists, and some pastors and teachers, for the equipping of the saints for the work of ministry, for the edifying of the body of Christ. (Ephesians 4:11–12)

One needs to understand spiritual gifts. Not everyone receives the same gift. Apostle Paul spoke about the variety of spiritual gifts and said not to be ignorant concerning spiritual gifts. Paul went on to say that there is a diversity of gifts but the same Spirit. There are differences in ministries, but the same Lord. And there is a diversity of activities, but it is the same God who works in all of them. The manifestation of the Spirit is given to each one for the profit of all (1 Corinthians 12:1:4–7). Paul added more by saying, "But the same Spirit works all these things, distributing to each one individually as He wills" (1 Corinthians 12:11). The purpose of these gifts is to equip the saints for the ministry's work: to edify the body of Christ (Ephesians 4:12). Furthermore, in Romans 12:4 and 6, the scripture states that "For as we have many members in one body, but all the members do not have the same function. Having gifts differing, according to the grace that is given to us, let us use them." God uses all gifts to accomplish His work in the world.

As I grew deeper in my faith in the Lord, my worldly desires vanished little by little. Everything I wanted on this earth seemed like a vapor. Earthly life was only temporary, and I could not take it to eternity. I started to pray the Lord's Prayer aloud daily, which can be found in Matthew 6:9–13.

> Our Father in Heaven,
> Hallowed be Your name.
> Your kingdom comes.
> Your will be done on earth as it is in Heaven.
> Give us this day our daily bread.
> And forgive us our debts,
> As we forgive our debtors.
> And do not lead us into temptation,
> But deliver us from the evil one.
> For Yours are the kingdom, the power, and
> the glory forever. Amen.

You may ask, why do I pray the Lord's Prayer? First, it's a prayer that the Lord Jesus taught His disciples to pray. Second, the Heavenly Father knows everything I need, therefore I should not pray long, windy prayers thinking that the Lord will be pleased. I should instead keep it short and straight to the point. Prayer is vital in Christian life. If you don't know what to pray, I suggest using the prayer that the Lord taught the disciples. Prayer is communication with God. You pray to request something from God; you give thanks, praises, and worship in prayer, but you should never neglect to stay still for God to speak to you as well. He speaks in a still, small voice; therefore, it is essential to keep silent after prayer. He may even talk to you in a dream, through your Christian friends, from reading the word of God in the Bible—there are various ways God can speak.

I wanted to know the heart of the Heavenly Father and His son Jesus. I asked the Holy Spirit to align my thoughts and ways to the ways and thoughts of my Heavenly Father. My Heavenly Father's ways and thoughts are higher than mine (Isaiah 55:9). I chose to walk the narrow path because the narrow path would produce a fruitful life with the Lord Jesus (Matthew 7:13-14). A narrow path meant a life focused on the teaching of Jesus, and not according to the world's view. This is what Matthew 7:13–14 says: "Enter by the narrow gate; for wide is the gate and broad is the way that leads to destruction, and there are many who go in by it. Because narrow is the gate and difficult is the way which leads to life, and there are few who find it."

I had the desire to share the good news of the Gospel to the lost world. Whenever I noticed people without any direction in life asking for advice, I took the opportunity to tell them the good news about Jesus. Jesus came to earth and died on the cross, and those who believe in Him will have life and have it more abundantly (John 10:10). The Heavenly Father so loved the world that He gave His one and only son, that whoever believes in Him shall not perish but have eternal life (John 3:16). And the most important message here is that the Heavenly Father sent His only begotten son to earth to die on the cross for the sins of people on this earth (John 3:16). We are all sinners and have fallen short of the glory of God (Romans 3:23). Wow! Isn't that good news? Our sins are forgiven, and the Lord came to give life and life more abundantly.

Do you wish to know more? The Lord further states in Matthew 11:28–30, "Come to Me, all you who labor and are heavy laden, and I will give you rest. Take My yoke upon you and learn from me, for I am gentle and lowly in heart, and you will find rest for your souls. For My yoke is easy, and My burden is light." Why does He say this? One thing we need to understand about Jesus is this: He is a loving God. He is a God who came down in human form to model the correct way of life, and who wanted to create a relationship with you and me. When God comes down to have a relationship with men, it is possible to hear God, walk with Him, and talk to Him. The Lord is your companion, and you can rely on Him during your difficult, stressful, chaotic life on earth. But how do you know that He is with you? It is crucial to understand why He had to die on the cross. Even though He died for your sins and mine, Jesus said in John 16:7, "Nevertheless I tell you the truth. It is to your advantage that I go away; for if I do not go away, the Helper will not come to you; but if I depart, I will send Him to you." In this passage, the Lord promises that the Holy Spirit will come and abide in believers after He has passed on.

Life in the hands of Jesus will lead one to a life of power in the Holy Spirit. The Holy Spirit will point to Jesus. Jesus stated in Matthew 16:13–14, "However, when He, the Spirit of truth, has come, He will guide you into all truth; for He will not speak on His own authority, but whatever He hears He will speak, and He will tell you things to come. He will glorify Me, for He will take of what is mine and declare it to you." When we confess and believe that Jesus is Lord, the Holy Spirit lives in us.

At this point, you are also a born-again Christian, which I mentioned earlier in this book. The moment you receive Jesus in your heart, you will be saved, and salvation is a gift from God. For some, feelings of guilt and shame may continue due to their way of living in the past, which was ugly in the sight of God. Yet the grace of God saves you from that past. Grace is essential for a Christ-believer, and one must gain the proper understanding of the subject of grace. Grace is unmerited favor (mercy) that our Heavenly Father gave to us by sending His one and only begotten son Jesus Christ to earth to die on the cross so that we could secure eternal salvation from sin. Grace is one of God's attributes, and because of grace, men do not need to earn salvation through good works; it is a gift from God. In Ephesians 2:8, the scripture states, "For by grace you have been saved through faith, and not of yourselves, it is the gift of God."

Does this mean you are changed overnight? Of course not. Transformation takes time, and that is the work of the Holy Spirit. The Holy Spirit will lead and guide you when you empty yourself and live a surrendered life. When you read the Bible, ask the Holy Spirit to give you understanding. He is your teacher. When you pray and do not know what to pray for, ask the Holy Spirit to help you pray. When you worship God, worship the Holy Spirit because He is God. There is only one God, but there are three in the Trinity, united in the Godhead of Christianity. The Trinity includes the Father, Son, and the Holy Spirit. The Holy Spirit in you will reveal the heart of Jesus and the Heavenly Father. The Heavenly Father and the Lord Jesus are in the third heaven, and you will not see them face-to face on earth. Therefore, the Holy Spirit will talk to you and lead your life into the perfection of the Lord Jesus (2 Corinthians 3:8). I do not despise people who have gone to Heaven, met Jesus face-to-face, and returned to earth to share their stories; the Lord has His ways to reveal Himself.

As for me, the Holy Spirit is my best friend, because Jesus states in John 15:15, "No longer do I call you servants, for a servant, does not know what his master is doing; but I have called you friends, for all things that I heard from My Father I have made known to you." I cling to Him with every breath. The Holy Spirit keeps me in tune with Jesus and the Heavenly Father. My mind and my heart are alert to God's presence and His power in transforming my life, as I intend to possess the mind and actions of Christ. The Holy Spirit is my secret to being alive with joy and peace. Even when I am in a difficult or stressful moment, I talk to my Lord, knowing what the Bible says about anxiousness. I pray and let my request be made known to God, and the peace of God, which surpasses every understanding, guards my heart and my mind through Christ Jesus (Philippians 4:6).

Walking with the Lord is exciting, and I have not experienced one moment of loneliness since I started my life with Jesus. High and low in every circumstance of life, I can overcome anything through the power of the Holy Spirit. Wow! What a powerful life! I see myself as a beautiful tree growing greener every day. My growth moves into holiness and godliness, pushing away things that the Lord dislikes. The Lord has brought me deeper into Him, and I desire to go even deeper with Him until one day I will see Him face-to-face in Heaven.

HOLDING ON TO JESUS
IN UNCERTAIN TIMES

I t is worrisome to see the chaotic state of this world. The coronavirus (COVID-19) has been the center of attention for quite a long time. Many lives have been lost, and it has been an unfortunate and devastating time. Working as a nurse in a hospital setting, I saw many patients being admitted with COVID-19. Many did not make it out of the hospital alive. What is even sadder is that the family is not allowed to visit during the patient's hospital stay unless the patient is profoundly sick or at the end of his or her life, never to go home again. The calls that came in from family members asking for an update on their loved ones were so desperate, anxious, and helpless. Some were frustrated and angry because they could not touch their family members, instead receiving only telephone updates from the direct care staff in the hospital. Even though many can get in touch via FaceTime, it is not the same as being present at the bedside with their loved ones.

COVID-19 has changed people's lives. The social distancing rules, daily symptoms checking, quarantining, businesses closing because of the virus, and even churches closing have caused many people to lose their jobs. As a nurse, it has been a hectic time at the hospital due to the overflow of COVID-19 patients. I thank God that I was able to keep my job. It has been a test, and my dependency on God increased like never before. I prayed before work each day, during working hours, and thanked God at each shift's end. I applied the blood of Jesus daily over my life by saying it aloud 'I apply the blood of Jesus over my life today', with faith for protection, but I also strictly adhered to all the guidelines that were put in place to protect me from being exposed to the virus.

It may sound strange that I apply the blood of Jesus when Jesus is not on earth physically. Going back to the Bible and the Old Testament, God instructed the people of Israel to apply the sacrificed lamb's blood on the doors of their houses. The blood on the doorpost was a sign that the people in that house were associated with God. When the angel of death came to kill the firstborn sons in the land of Egypt, the doorposts with the blood were bypassed. No plague came over those houses. The blood from the lamb killed, roasted, and eaten signified the Lord's Passover (Exodus12:3-13). The Israelites would not have been protected if the blood were not applied to the doors of their houses.

Meanwhile, in the New Testament, Jesus is the true Passover lamb. The Lord Jesus came to earth and died on the cross. His body was broken, and His blood was shed on the cross. The blood of Jesus marks those who believe by faith that Jesus is the son of God and died for our sins on the cross, and they escape eternal death. In other words, we, the believers who symbolically apply the blood of Jesus to our hearts, cause God's judgment to pass over us sinners and give us everlasting life (Hebrews 10:14 and Romans 6:23). Satan cannot stand the blood of Jesus if we confess it aloud for protection. We confess it aloud because life and death are in the power of the tongue (Proverbs 18:21). Therefore, for one of the ways to experience victory over evil, the blood of Jesus is required, and we need to confess it with our mouths. In short, I apply the blood of Jesus daily over my life for protection.

When I am at work, I silently pray in my heart for all my patients, including their family members who are not there. At one time, this was overwhelming due to the overflow of patients, and I grieved at the number of patients who died and the families who suffered deeply due to the loss of their loved ones. One day, while I was off duty, I was exhausted and could hardly bear the devastating situation that we faced. I set apart time on that off day just by myself for prayer, and I called down Heaven to intervene for us. I said, "Lord, you must come down now and stop the spread of the virus." I shouted aloud, asking Him to forgive our sins and wash them away with the blood of Jesus. I told Him I could not take this anymore and asked the Lord to please help us. I was feeling disappointed that God had not intervened after so many lives had been taken. I told the Lord, "You have all the answers about everything that is happening on this earth, and I beg You to do something for us here." I also reminded the Lord, "Nothing is impossible in Your hands, so why can't You stop it?" Humbly I surrendered my prayer into the hands of God because God is in control of everything.

I continued working, knowing my Lord is my strength

in my weakness. The Lord's grace was sufficient for me. As the days went by, the number of COVID-19 patients being admitted lessened. I thanked God for that. What was surprising was the number decreased to less than 50 percent in two weeks. The overflow unit was closed. In my heart, I was overjoyed; it was good news to all of us. The vaccine was out, and the entire staff got vaccinated; the entire nation was getting vaccinated as well. After one month, the number of patients with COVID-19 was fewer than ten in our hospital. I said to myself, "This seems too good to be true," then I recalled the prayer I'd spoken a few weeks ago. I asked myself, *Did the Lord hear me calling Him down to help us?*

I remembered the scripture in Genesis 18:24–32.

> "Suppose there were fifty righteous within the city; would You also destroy the place and not spare it for the fifty righteous people in it? Far be it from You to do such a thing as this, to slay the righteous with the wicked, so that the righteous should be as the wicked; far be it from You! Shall not the Judge of all the earth do, right?" So, the LORD said, "If I find in Sodom fifty righteous within the city, then I will spare all the place for their sakes." Then Abraham answered and said, "Indeed now, I who am but dust and ashes have taken it upon myself to speak to the Lord: Suppose there were five less than the fifty righteous; would You destroy all the city for lack of five?" So, He said, "If I find there forty-five,

I will not destroy it." And he spoke to Him yet again and said, "Suppose there should be forty found there?" So, He said, "I will not do it for the sake of forty." Then he said, "Let not the Lord be angry, and I will speak: Suppose thirty should be found there?" So, He said, "I will not do it if I find thirty there." And He said, "Indeed now, I have taken it upon myself to speak to the Lord: Suppose twenty should be found there?" So, He said, "I will not destroy it for the sake of twenty." Then he said, "Let not the Lord be angry, and I will speak but once more: Suppose ten should be found there?" And He said, "I will not destroy it for the sake of ten."

I learned a valuable lesson: God hears the prayers of His people during disastrous times. I am sure many people from my church prayed at home, and God heard their prayers and intervened on their behalf. Though some may say that the vaccine is the reason the number decreased, deep in my heart, I know God heard our righteous prayers and spared our lives. I relate my prayer to the scripture from Genesis, where it is proven that God is the same yesterday, today, and forever (Hebrews 13:8). This is how life in the hands of Jesus is: He is a God of love, full of compassion, never changing, ever-faithful, all-powerful, and merciful. I can go on with a lengthy list, but above all, He is a living God.

MY DESTINY IN THE HANDS OF JESUS

Even though I plan for my future, I surrender my plans into the hands of Jesus. Jesus knows what's best for my life. One of the attributes of the Lord Jesus is His omniscience: He knows everything. He knows our past, present, and future. How do I know that the Lord knows my past? I know it from the scripture, where Jesus encountered a woman from Samaria in John 4:16–19. Jesus said to her,

> "Go, call your husband, and come here." The woman answered and said, "I have no husband." Jesus said to her, "You have well said, 'I have no husband.' For you have had five husbands, and the one whom you now have is not your husband; in that, you spoke truly." The woman said to Him, "Sir, I perceive that You are a prophet."

Therefore, I know the Lord knows my past. He knows what we are doing now because the Holy Spirit is in us. Jesus knew that one of His disciples, Judas, would betray

Him for thirty pieces of silver. The scripture is found in John 13:21–27.

> When Jesus had said these things, He was troubled in Spirit, testified, and said, "Most assuredly, I say to you, one of you will betray Me." Then the disciples looked at one another, perplexed about whom He spoke. Now there was leaning on Jesus' bosom one of His disciples, whom Jesus loved. Simon Peter, therefore, motioned to him to ask who it was of whom He spoke. Then, leaning back on Jesus' breast, he said to Him, "Lord, who is it?" Jesus answered, "It is he to whom I shall give a piece of bread when I have dipped it." And having dipped the bread, He gave it to Judas Iscariot, the son of Simon. Now, after the piece of bread, Satan entered him. Then Jesus said to him, "What you do, do quickly."

Jesus knows the very things we will do right now. He knows what we will do in the future and everything that is to come. In John 13:36–38, He foretells His disciple Peter's denial about knowing Him.

> Simon Peter said to Him, "Lord, where are You going?" Jesus answered him, "Where I am going, you cannot follow Me now, but you shall follow Me afterward." Peter said to Him, "Lord, why can I not follow You now? I will lay down my life for Your

sake." Jesus answered him, "Will you lay down your life for My sake? I say to you; the rooster shall not crow till you have denied Me three times."

Peter did deny Jesus three times soon after because he was fearful for his life and feared he would be persecuted with Jesus. Jesus already knew what was coming and what Peter would do. That is the reason I trust that my destiny is in the hands of Jesus.

It is exciting to be with Jesus; by surrendering everything into Him, the ride is filled with suspense and adventure. That is how I perceive my future: I do not know what is coming, but the Lord knows. The most important thing is to be led by the Holy Spirit. For as many as are led by the Spirit of God, these are sons of God (Romans 8:14). To ensure the Spirit of God drives you, the first thing you must do is acknowledge the Lord when you wake up in the morning. Thank Him for waking you and sparing your life. Prayer, worship, and reading the Word of God are essential in Christian life to ensure your life is directed to the Lord's path for you. Therefore, seek first the kingdom of God and His righteousness, and all these things shall be added to you (Matthew 6:33). The close connection you have with God will enable you to sense the timing of heaven on earth. The passage in Ecclesiastes 3:1 says, "For everything, there is a season. A time for every purpose under Heaven." Every up and down, stressful and difficult moment, failure, and every success and sweet event in this life is a lesson to be learned. When we experience trials in life, they strengthen our inner being, and that is how God molds us to be the person He wants us to be. He is the author and finisher of our faith (Hebrews 12:12). I promise you will finish strong when you walk intimately with God each day. The Word of God says all things work together for good to those who love God, to those who are called according to His purpose (Romans 8:28). God is a faithful God (1 Corinthians 1:9).

LIFE AFTER DEATH
WITH JESUS

H e has risen! What do I mean by that sentence? Outside of Jerusalem, at Golgotha, Jesus was crucified on a tree with two other thieves because He claimed to be the king of the Jews. After His death on that cross, His body was wrapped in a clean linen cloth and placed in a tomb with a large stone rolled across to close it. The tomb was secured and sealed, and a guard set. The day He died was a Friday. On the third day, Sunday morning, Mary Magdalene, accompanied by the other Mary, came to see the tomb and found it empty. The stone was rolled away; seated on the stone was an angel. The angel told them not to be afraid because Jesus had risen. This passage of resurrection is from Matthew 28:1–10.

> After the Sabbath, as the first day of the week began to dawn, Mary Magdalene and the other Mary came to see the tomb. And behold, there was a great earthquake; for an angel of the Lord descended from Heaven and came and rolled back the stone from

the door and sat on it. His countenance was like lightning, and his clothing as white as snow. And the guards shook for fear of Him and became like dead men. But the angel answered and said to the women, "Do not be afraid, for I know that you seek Jesus who was crucified. He is not here, for He is risen, as He said. Come, see the place where the Lord lay. And go quickly and tell His disciples that He has risen from the dead, and indeed He is going before you into Galilee; there you will see Him. Behold, I have told you." And as they went to tell His disciples, behold, Jesus met them, saying, "Rejoice!" So, they came and held Him by the feet and worshiped Him. Then Jesus said to them, "Do not be afraid. Go and tell My brethren to go to Galilee, and there they will see Me."

This crucial passage is from Bible itself and forms the foundation of the Christian faith. Jesus did not just die on the cross for our sins to be forgiven but arose from the dead to inform us that we will also rise again after death. As Christians who follows Jesus's footsteps, our bodies will rise again after we die. In other words, the resurrection of Christ shows us what is to come after we leave this earth.

According to the apostle Paul in 1 Corinthians 15:20–22, "But now Christ is risen from the dead, and has become the first fruits of those who have fallen asleep. For since by Man came death, by Man also came the resurrection of the death. For as in Adam all die, even so in Christ all shall be made alive." Those in Christ will be made alive and spend eternity with Jesus in Heaven.

Eternal life is mentioned many times in the Bible. I want to share some of them here.

> "And I give them eternal life, and they shall never perish; neither shall anyone snatch them out of My hand. My Father, who gave them to Me, is greater than all; and no one can snatch them out of My Father's hand. My Father and I are one."(John 10:28–30)

> And this is the testimony: that God has given us eternal life, and this life is in His Son. (1 John 5:11)

> For God so loved the world that He gave His only begotten Son, that whoever believes in Him should not perish but have everlasting life. (John 3:16)

> For the wages of sin is death, but the gift of God is eternal life in Christ Jesus our Lord. (Romans 6:23)

> He who believes in the Son has everlasting life, and he who does not believe the Son shall not see life, but the wrath of God abides on him. (John 3:36)

In conclusion, whoever believes that Jesus died on the cross for our sins and rose again on the third day, will spend the rest of their lives after death with the Lord Jesus in Heaven. In other words, it simply means we will live forever as our Lord Jesus does.

The resurrection of Christ on the third day is what impacted me the most. I have mentioned earlier in this book that I had a tremendous fear about dying and many burning questions of what will happen after death. The most comforting scripture for me is found in John 14:1–4: "Let not your heart be troubled; you believe in God, also believe in Me. In My Father's house are many mansions; if it were not so, I would have told you. I go to prepare a place for you. And if I go and prepare a place for you, I will come again and receive you to Myself; where I am, there you may also be. And where I go, you know, and the way you know." In the hands of Jesus, there is a living hope. What a savior He is!

MY JESUS IS A JUST GOD

As I experience a deeper relationship with the lover of my soul, it is crucial to know that He is a just God. A just God means that He is fair and impartial. He can be called a judge in another name. The Lord Jesus will judge a person's wrong and right doings. The Lord will conduct justice according to His standards. The Lord's ways and thoughts are much higher than human thoughts (Isaiah 55:8–9). The Lord urges us not to be conformed to this world but to be transformed by the renewing of the mind through the Word of God (Romans 12:2). Our Lord Jesus is like our earthly or biological father or mother, who corrects a child behaving inappropriately. My biological dad was a loving person, but at the same time, he was firm in correcting my wrongdoing. My dad taught me to respect and speak politely to everyone. If I disrespected anyone, my dad would raise his voice and instruct me not to talk in such a way, correcting me at that very moment. This is an example of how a dad teaches or instructs a child to behave properly. Our Heavenly Father gave us the Word of God as a lamp to our feet and a light to our path (Psalm 119:105), to teach, correct, and master a godly lifestyle. Additionally, in 2 Timothy 3:16–17, the Word of God says, "All scripture is given by inspiration of God, and is profitable for doctrine, for reproof, for correction, for instruction in righteousness, that the man of God may be complete, thoroughly equipped for every good work."

Even though we have eternal life with God in Heaven, as a child of God, we must be aware that there will be a Judgment Day once the body is resurrected after death. I mention this because the apostle Paul told his readers in Philippians 2:12 "to work out your salvation with fear and trembling." The Lord is shaping us to be obedient to His way through the process of sanctification. Jesus is known as a merciful and gracious God, but at the same time, He is a just God who will judge you according to the way you have lived your life on earth. He wants us to pursue holiness and godliness because God is holy Himself (Leviticus 19:2). Holiness is the nature of God. Holiness will keep you from the unfruitful, destroying ways of today's generation in this current world.

Life in the hands of Jesus is perfection because He wants His children to be holy, blameless, and without a spot when we finally see Him face-to-face in Heaven. The secret to this transformation is via the Holy Spirit living in us once we receive the Lord into our hearts. Ask the Holy Spirit to lead you to walk in the Spirit.

We must also spend time reading and meditating on the Word of God daily. By doing so, we will gradually walk in the Spirit and not in fulfilling the lust of the flesh. What is the difference between living in the Spirit of God and the flesh? The fleshly work includes adultery, fornication, uncleanness, licentiousness, idolatry, sorcery, hatred, contentions, jealousy, outbursts of wrath, selfish ambitions, and dissension heresies, envy, murders, drunkenness, revelries, and the like. Those who practice such things will not inherit the kingdom of God, which means they will not be the heirs to eternal life (Galatians 5:19–21).

The Spirit's fruit is love, joy, peace, longsuffering, kindness, goodness, faithfulness, gentleness, and self-control (Galatians 5:22–23). Longsuffering means to be patient in facing hardship in all circumstances that we face on earth. Therefore, ask the Holy Spirit to help you walk in the Spirit daily. God, in his loving kindness and mercy, wants us to be transformed, to be Christ like. It takes a lifetime journey to be perfected like the Lord Jesus.

In the hands of Jesus, there is a high calling for one to be moving away from the wicked way of living and to become righteous in every aspect of life. One must be aware that hell is mentioned by the Lord Jesus many times in the Bible. Only those whose names are found in the Book of Life will be going to Heaven. Those whose names are not found in that Book of Life will be thrown into the lake of fire (Revelation 20:15). You cannot manipulate God for your personal gain. When you use God's name for popularity and money, you must be fearful of God's wrath. You will be troubled on Judgment Day when your body is resurrected.

The scripture from Matthew 7:21–23 states:

> "Not everyone who says to Me, 'Lord, Lord,' shall enter the kingdom of Heaven, but he who does the will of My Father in Heaven. Many will say to Me in that day, 'Lord, Lord, have we not prophesied in Your name, cast out demons in Your name, and

done many wonders in Your name?' And then I will declare to them, 'I never knew you; depart from Me, you who practice lawlessness!'"

In Matthew 21:12–13, it says, "Then Jesus went into the temple of God and drove out all those who bought and sold in the temple and overturned the tables of the money-changers and the seats of those who sold doves. And He said to them, 'It is written, "My house shall be called a house of prayer," but you have made it a den of thieves.'"

I am not pointing fingers at anyone on this particular subject, but if anyone intends to sell the name of Jesus for profit in any kind, the Lord will not be pleased. Another scripture from Revelation 3:16 says, "So then because you are lukewarm, and neither cold nor hot, I will spew you out of My mouth." The Lord wants us to walk with Him in total faithfulness by keeping our minds and hearts focused on Him.

I am even more in love with my Lord Jesus because He is fair in judging His people. He dislikes liars, compromisers, hypocrites, idolaters, and those who live by the world's corrupted, fleshly desires. The Lord knows everything in a person's heart and judges righteously and not as people do. People look at the outward appearance, but the Lord looks at the heart (1 Samuel 16:7). In Acts 5:1–11, Ananias and Sapphira died instantly after lying to the Holy Spirit regarding money matters. Below is the full scripture.

But a certain man named Ananias, with Sapphira, his wife, sold a possession. And he kept back part of the proceeds, his wife also being aware of it, and brought a certain part and laid it at the apostles' feet. But Peter said, "Ananias, why has Satan filled your heart to lie to the Holy Spirit and keep back part of the price of the land for yourself? While it remained, was it not your own? And after it was sold, was it not in your own control? Why have you conceived this thing in your heart? You have not lied to men but God." Then Ananias, hearing these words, fell and breathed his last. So great fear came upon all those who heard these things. And the young men arose and wrapped him up, carried him out, and buried him. Now it was about three hours later when his wife came in, not knowing what had happened. And Peter answered her, "Tell me whether you sold the land for so much?" She said, "Yes, for so much." Then Peter said to her, "How is it that you have agreed together to test the Spirit of the Lord? Look, the feet of those who have buried your husband are at the door, and they will carry you out." Then immediately, she fell at his feet and breathed her last. And the young men came in and found her dead, and carrying her out, buried her by her husband. So great fear came upon all the church and upon all who heard these things.

I am looking forward to being perfected by my Lord. Heaven and Hell are a reality for Christians. Some were brought up to Heaven, and some sent to Hell but came back to share their experiences on this earth. I have not had any of these experiences, but the Holy Spirit that lives in me confirms it through the reading of the Word of God from the Bible.

THE LORD IS MY DWELLING PLACE

E ver since I became the child of God some years back, I yearned to dwell in the house of my Lord Jesus. In John 1:12–13, the apostle John said, "But like many, as received Him, to them He gave the right to become children of God, to those who believe in His name: who were born, not of blood, nor the will of the flesh, nor the will of man, but of God." From that verse, one should acknowledge that whoever receives Christ Jesus into his or her heart is born again. As a newly born-again Christian, I started my life as a baby in the hands of Jesus. I felt His love showered over me. As a baby Christian, I was eager to learn about my Jesus in the Bible; I asked questions about prayer, worship, understanding the Bible, the Holy Spirit, fasting, and many more things. I asked for explanations from the pastor of my church and from my Christian mates, listened to sermons, read a Bible with a concordance, and always thought about my Jesus and His ways of living.

As I grew in my Christian walk, I came to know my Jesus more. I knew His likes and dislikes, His voice, and His presence. The Word of God did say that "My sheep hear My voice, and I know them, and they follow Me" (John 10:27). Walking intimately with my Lord made me sensitive to His presence, and I was cautious not to offend the dearest lover of my soul. In Ephesians 4:30–32, the scripture touches on grieving the Holy Spirit:

> And do not grieve the Holy Spirit of God, by whom you were sealed for the day of redemption. Let all bitterness, wrath, anger, clamor, and evil speaking be put away from you, with all malice. And be kind to one another, tenderhearted, forgiving one another, even as God in Christ forgave you.

Forgiveness is vital in a Christian walk with God. If I do not forgive others' wrongdoing, my Heavenly Father would not forgive me of my sin either (Matthew 6:15). Therefore, I make it a point not to keep any bitterness or unforgiveness of others in my heart. By letting go of the grudge and unforgiveness, I know my Heavenly Father will listen to my prayer, and I can continue walking with Him peacefully, growing with my Lord to be more Christlike and finally into perfection of His Son, Jesus Christ. These three scriptures below are the reminder of unforgiveness if ever I have it in my heart:

> "For if you forgive men their trespasses, your Heavenly Father will also forgive you. But if you do not forgive men their trespasses, neither will your Father forgive your trespasses." Matthew 6:14–15

> "Therefore, if you bring your gift to the altar, and there remember that your brother has something against you, leave your gift there before the altar, and go your way. First, be reconciled to your brother, and then come and offer your gift." (Matthew 5:23–24)

> Then Peter came to Him and said, "Lord, how often shall my brother sin against me, and I forgive him? Up to seven times?" Jesus said to him, "I do not say to you, up to seven times, but up to seventy times seven." Matthew 18:21–22

My body is the dwelling place for my Lord. Therefore, forgiveness is a crucial factor that makes me walk freely with Jesus. The apostle Paul said in 1 Corinthians 6:19, "Or do you not know that your body is the temple of the Holy Spirit who is in you, whom you have from God, and you are not your own?" Isn't that fascinating that God's permanent dwelling place is in the believer's temple (body)? The scripture from John 14:16–17 confirms this; Jesus said, "And I will pray for the Father, and He will give you another Helper, that He may abide with you forever, even the Spirit of truth, whom the world cannot receive because it neither sees Him nor knows Him; but you know Him, for He dwells with you and will be in you."

When God lives in me, I live in the presence of God, and His power works in me. That indicates I have the mind of Christ. Instead of looking for a place where the Lord can be found, He came down to earth to have a relationship with

His believers and live in the temple of His beloved. Since my body is the dwelling place of God, I make sure to walk in His ways, where holiness and purity of my heart and mind must be exercised. "Surely goodness and mercy shall follow me all the days of my life, and I will dwell in the house of the Lord forever and ever" (Psalm 23:6).

I want to share a beautiful expression from David in the book of Psalms, found in the Old Testament:

> The Lord is my shepherd; I shall not want. He makes me lie down in green pastures; He leads me beside the still waters. He restores my soul; He leads me in the paths of righteousness for His name's sake. Yea, though I walk through the valley of the shadow of death, I will fear no evil; For You are with me; Your rod and Your staff, they comfort me. You prepare a table before me in the presence of my enemies; You anoint my head with oil; My cup runs over. Surely goodness and mercy shall follow me all the days of my life, And I will dwell in the house of the Lord Forever. (Psalm 23:1–6)

Life in the hands of Jesus is secured because He is there in the valley of the shadow of death, and He protects me in the presence of my enemies. I never stand alone during difficulty or sorrowful moments. The Lord is always there with me and in me. I memorized Psalm 23 in my heart. I say it out loud during my prayer time.

WORDS FROM MY JESUS

My Lord said, "What is the benefit of gaining the entire world, but you lose your own soul at the end?" (Matthew 16:26). The world has a unique attraction that makes people fall in love with it. Humans are drawn towards money, fame, power, and the material things the world has to offer. Yet, after all, it is only temporal and cannot be taken into eternity. It is a clever idea to leave a legacy behind for your loved ones, but it is even better to have the blessing of the Almighty God in everything that you leave behind and continue life into eternity with God.

Every person on earth will love you for a season or a reason, but the love of God is eternal. Every single person you love on earth will leave you someday when the end of life comes, but life in the hands of God is eternal life. The stuff you possess can get old and rusty and may need a replacement one day, but having Jesus in life never fades. He is the everlasting beauty; He is the Alpha and Omega; nothing compares to Him. Be cautious when craving more and more stuff and remaining unsatisfied. It might mean one is greedy, or it might be Satan is tempting you. In Matthew 4:8–11, Jesus was tested by the devil.

Again, the devil took Him up on an exceedingly high mountain and showed Him all the kingdoms of the world and their glory. And he said to Him, "All these things I will give You if You fall and worship me." Then Jesus said to him, "Away with you, Satan! For it is written, 'You shall worship the Lord your God, and Him only you shall serve.'" Then the devil left Him, and behold, angels, came and ministered to Him.

One will not be shaken in the hands of God; He knew you before you were formed in your mother's womb (Jeremiah 1:5). He has a plan and a purpose for you on earth; He will lead you and guide you to fulfill that purpose. He will bless you and your descendants. The Lord came to give you a more abundant life (John 10:10). Jesus protects His people, and He gives His angels charge over you (Psalm 91:11–12). Life in the hands of Jesus is a powerful life because the Holy Spirit lives in us. God is generous in wisdom, and therefore He gives it to everyone who asks for wisdom (James 1:5). Wisdom is required in every aspect of life on earth.

In summary, life in the hands of Jesus is a complete life that brings every aspect of our lives into completion and perfection, after which we will meet Jesus face-to-face in Heaven and spend the rest of eternity with Him.

My heart's desire is for everyone to experience this special love. It is our nature as humans to be loved and to share that love with someone else. It is a special feeling that no words can describe. Only those who have experienced a broken relationship know what it is to be broken-hearted.

In my journey of being a single woman, I was hungry and desperate to be loved by a man in my younger years. I had a deep desire to marry and have a family of my own—but everything changed when I was thirty-four. Life took a 360-degree turn. My lover, the Lord Jesus Himself, found me. He revealed His heart to me, and ever since then I have been deeply in love with Him. I am still asking for more of Him every day. No one can take that place in my heart but Jesus, and Jesus only. I am complete in Him, and there is no other that I look for anymore. It does not mean that you will be like me, single in your life, but God has everything planned in His book. He knows the right partner for your life, and He will bring it to pass in His perfect timing.

Wherever you are in the walk of your life, Jesus is waiting, and He is knocking at the door of your heart. In Revelation 3:20, Jesus said, "Behold, I stand at the door and knock. If anyone hears My voice and opens the door, I will come into Him and dine with him, and he with Me." Jesus loves to have a relationship with us on earth. Your new life will start by confessing these words aloud: "Lord Jesus, I believe you are the son of God. You died on the cross for my sins, and you rose on the third day. Come into my heart Lord Jesus and be the Lord and Savior of my life from now on." From now on experience the love and life transformation that will take place in your life.

In Romans 3:23, the Word of God says that we all have sinned and fallen short of the glory of God. Furthermore, the Lord Jesus said in John 14:6, "I am the way, the truth, and the life. No one comes to the Father except through Me." I can prove to you that Jesus is the way, the truth, and the life. As a child growing up in a Hindu belief system, I questioned the existence of God. Coming from a society of diverse beliefs in Malaysia, I was exposed to different religions and had the opportunity to learn about God. But the one true God stood up among all the other beliefs or so-called religions and touched my heart. He gave His presence, and spoke to me in a still, small voice, "I am He the one living God that you been looking for." I met Jesus in church and the rest is history. May the Lord bless you and keep you. Amen.

Printed in the United States
by Baker & Taylor Publisher Services